CARTOONS *for the* CHAOS

CARTOONS *for the* CHAOS

Poems 1975 – 2025

Richard Collins

SHANTI ARTS PUBLISHING

BRUNSWICK, MAINE

CARTOONS for the CHAOS

Published by Shanti Arts LLC

193 Hillside Road
Brunswick, Maine 04011

shantiarts.com

Designed by Shanti Arts Designs

Printed in the United States of America

ISBN: 978-1-971191-02-7 (softcover)

to agelasts everywhere

CONTENTS

ACKNOWLEDGMENTS ... 11

PREFACE

STAGES ON LIFE'S WAY ... 21

FACES

SERIOUS INQUIRIES ONLY ... 25
REARRANGING THINGS YOU SAID ... 28
NAKED NOT NUDE ... 30
IS THAT A LANDSCAPE OUT MY WINDOW? ... 31
THIS DEGRADATION ... 32
THE MUSIC OF SNAPDRAGONS IS FRAGRANT ... 34
THE NOVELIST ON THE CARPET ... 35
CEUX-CI NE SONT PAS DES POÈMES D'AMOUR ... 36
TONIGHT THE VODKA TASTES LIKE CHOCOLATE ... 37
THE WOMAN AT THE PARTY WITH HER ENTOURAGE ... 38
WHO LOVES THE FROG? ... 42
BLATANCIES OF WHALEBONE ... 43
SHE CHANNELS HER LATE FATHER BY SHARING
   HIS RECORD COLLECTION ON TIKTOK ... 44
CANNIBAL AFFECTATIONS ... 46
VIRGIN BRIDES AND TENNIS PLAYERS ... 47
APATHETIC PANTOUMERY ... 48
THE SWEETNESS OF LIFE ... 50

PLACES

OFTEN I STOP IN MID-SENTENCE, RECALL ... 55
HERE, HALFWAY ... 56
FORTY AIN'T SO BAD ... 57
MACOMBER, FRANCIS AND HIS ELEGIAC DANCES ... 58
NIGHTWATCHMAN READS BECKETT ON PROUST ... 59
SLEEPLESS IN CUERNAVACA ... 60
THE HAUNTING OF HOUSES ... 61
MOVING DAY ... 63
THE NEW BUCHAREST ... 65

AN AMERICAN SOCIOLOGIST IN ROMANIA   66
THE MOVING VANS MARKED METAPHOR   67
THINGS WE NOTICED IN THE TAVERNA   68
THE WAITER   69
DREAMING OF EUCALYPTUS   70
SAPPHO'S ELEPHANT   71
INTERREGNUM: OR THE STONE OPERATION   72
HOLLYWOOD   75

DISGRACES

THANKS, IT'S GOOD FRIDAY IN FAIRFAX COUNTY   79
NOVEMBER 2024   80
JANUARY 2026   81
DA WABBIT WACE   82
BUGS BUNNY, POSTMODERN POSTMORTEM   83
HYPOTHESIS WITH LITTLE SYMBOLISM
     AND LESS SCIENCE   84
STILL LIFE WITH WAR   85
STUDY FOR A MASSACRE OF THE INNOCENTS   86
WATCHING SNOW FALL IN UKRAINE   88
OBSESSED WITH THE NEWS AT BREAKFAST   89
WHY MY CAT IS NAMED HITLER   90
I WANT TO WRITE A POEM THAT RHYMES JESUS   91
SOMETIMES SOMETIMES IS NOW   92
SOMETIMES OUR HUMAN   93
JERUSALEM SYNDROME   94
THE RUDE OLD GUY AT THE U-HAUL DROP-OFF
     IN BOULDER   97
POSTHUMANIST PROTAGORAS   99
PARADE OF ONCE WELL-REGARDED DEMONS   101

TRACES

SPITTING IMAGES   107
IDIOSYNCRATIC ICONS: A MANIFESTO   109
CAUTIONARY SONG   111
THE ELEPHANT MEMORY   112
REPETITION IS AN ELEPHANT   113

JUBILATE ELEPHANTI 114
SMALL TOWN CLASSIFIED 116
THE GUY WHO NOW READS ONLY
    FINNEGANS WAKE 117
THE GIRL ON THE SWING IN THE CASINO 119
RICTUS SARDONICUS PLAYS SOLITAIRE
    IN THE DARK 120
THE HUBRIS OF INTENTIONAL DEFECT 122
THE WHEEL AND THE BALL 123
DECOMPOSITION 125
THE UPSIDE OF CLIMATE CHANGE 126
TORNADO WARNING 127
BORN IN 1952 129
A CERTAINTY 130

POSTFACE

THE AROMA OF ANGELS 135

ABOUT THE AUTHOR 137

IMAGES

The image that appears on the cover of this book along with those at the beginning of each section are from *Kyōsai's Pictures of One Hundred Demons*. The artist, Kawanabe Kyōsai (1831–1889), whose name also appears as Kawanabe Gyōsai, was described by art historian Timothy Clark as the "last virtuoso in traditional Japanese painting." Kyōsai is also considered to be Japan's first political caricaturist, having been arrested several times and even imprisoned for the political nature of his work.

Kyōsai's Pictures of One Hundred Demons was published soon after his death in 1889. The images were made from woodblocks and printed with ink on paper. The collection is in the holdings of The Metropolitan Museum of Art in New York City.

ACKNOWLEDGMENTS

Thanks to the editors of the following journals in which these poems appeared in their original forms:

300 Days of Sun: "Hypothesis with Little Symbolism and Less Science" (2024)

Abbey: "Is That a Landscape Out My Window?" (1990)

Angel's Flight: "Interregnum, or The Stone Operation" (1976)

Aphor: "Rearranging Things You Said" and "Sleepless in Cuernavaca" (2025)

Azure: A Journal of Literary Thought: "Idiosyncratic Icons: A Manifesto" and "Repetition Is an Elephant" (2025)

Bad Haircut Quarterly: "Why My Cat Is Named Hitler" (1989)

Balestra Magazine: "Nightwatchman Reads Beckett on Proust" (2026)

BarBar: "Naked Not Nude" and "Sappho's Elephant" (2024)

Beautiful Little Fools—A Broken Spine slimline anthology (United Kingdom): "The Girl on the Swing in the Casino" and "The Woman at the Party with Her Entourage" (2025)

Big Bridge: Sturm und Drang: "Cannibal Affectations" and "Cautionary Song" (2009)

Blue Violin: "Stages on Life's Way" and "The Waiter" (2000)

Chiron Review: "Rearranging Things You Said" (1991)

Clockhouse: "November 2024." (2025; nominated for Pushcart Prize)

Constance: Delicate Burdens: "Da Wabbit Wace" (2008)

#Genocidal—Culture Cult Press anthology: "Jerusalem Syndrome" and "Still Life with War" (2025)

Fell Swoop: "The Music of Snapdragons Is Fragrant" (c. 1992)

Five Fleas: "Born in 1952" (2025)

Hogtown Creek Review: "Bugs Bunny, Postmodern Postmortem" (2000)

The Hooghly Review: "The Guy Who Now Reads Only Finnegans Wake" (2025)

Impetus 2: "Personal: Good old country boy" (1990)

New Verse News: "January 2026" (2026)

Northridge Review: "Still Life with War" and "Study for Massacre of the Innocents" (2024)

Penelle Magazine: "A Zippered Bible Bound in Fake Leather" (2025)

The Plentitudes: "Spitting Images" (2024)

Sisyphus: "Here, Halfway" (1990)

Spillway: "The Moving Vans Marked Metaphor" (1997)

Syzygy: "The Elephant Memory"; "The Hubris of Defect"; "Posthumanist Protagoras"; and "The Upside of Climate Change" (2025)

Thirteen Poetry Magazine: "Forty Ain't So Bad"; "Macomber, Francis and His Elegiac Dances"; and "Thanks, It's Good Friday in Fairfax County" (1994)

This Degradation (New Sins): "This Degradation" and "Why My Cat Is Named Hitler" (1992)

Thus Spake the Corpse: An Exquisite Corpse Reader 1988-1998, 2 vols., Black Sparrow Press: "An American Sociologist in Romania"; "The Aroma of Angels"; "The New Bucharest"; and "The Sweetness of Life" (1999-2000)

Tickets to Midnight: "I Want to Write a Poem that Rhymes Jesus" (2025)

Vice Versa: "This Degradation" (1990)

Willawaw Journal: "Dreaming of Eucalyptus" (2024)

Wordsworth's Socks: "Serious Inquiries Only" (1988)

YAWP: "The Wheel and the Ball" (2004)

Zest of the Lemon: "Small Town Classified" (2025)

Cartoon: [kahr-toon] n. (from Italian, *cartone*, and Dutch, *karton*–describing strong heavy paper or pasteboard as in "carton"): 1) a full-scale drawing or design made on sturdy paper as a model for a painting, fresco, stained glass, tapestry, etc.; 2) a sketch or drawing, often humorous or satirical, symbolizing or caricaturing some topic or person; 3) an animated film for children or adults.

Chaos: [kay-oss] n. (from Greek, *khaos*, a vast chasm or void): 1) in Greek mythology, the first created being, from which came the primeval deities, Gaia, Tartarus, Erebus, and Nyx; 2) a gaping abyss, later the formless primordial matter; 3) in physics, behavior so unpredictable as to appear random; 4) utter confusion, disorder.

Preface

A MAN, PERHAPS THE ARTIST HIMSELF, HAS
SET DOWN HIS CALLIGRAPHY BRUSH AND
REACHES TO EXTINGUISH A LAMP. ONCE
DARKNESS FALLS, THE DEMONS WILL APPEAR.

STAGES ON LIFE'S WAY

I wanted to write poems epic in scale
with ink distilled from the charcoal remains
of Gutenbergs penned with cormorants' quills
on paper the size of trireme sails.

I wanted to write sonnets, no, not perfect
sonnets, but poems pretty as the press
of a thigh in a swing in a painting by
Boucher on mauve paper soft
as the bellies of newborn mice.

I wanted to write a check on an ice cube
I could cash in the middle of September
in the midst of a major U.S. city
without a credit card, passport, or any
form of accepted I.D.

I wanted to write an epigram, just one,
to be remembered, on the butt of a gun
or the button of a baseball cap.

I wanted to write something, sometime,
somewhere, something about faces and places,
disgraces and their traces, for someone
who might give a damn. Why not now?
Being of sound mind,
why not now?

Faces

AT LEFT, A MONSTER HOLDS UP A MIRROR FOR AN
OTAFUKU-ESQUE GHOUL TO APPLY BLACK DYE TO
HER TEETH. AT RIGHT, A CHUBBY FACED FIGURE
CARRIES A BAG BESIDE A THREE-EYED GHOUL.

SERIOUS INQUIRIES ONLY

—poems found in the personals

Not available in any bar
—only through this ad.
Looks don't matter
Race unimportant
Age, weight, children OK
No marital intentions
Reply with your desires.

1.

I'm a white widow in her 70s
& too much life for my age.
That's why I'd like to meet
someone who does not hang in bars
or use drugs to share my life.
I love home, little trips, nice
music. I'm clean & a little old
fashioned. I'd like a mature man
who doesn't sit & sleep in front of TV.

2.

Most people say I'm dull
yet I believe I'm just
a quiet & lonely type of guy
looking for a homely type of gal.

If you are 5'3" or above
& 140# or below
with green eyes & good bones
you could wrap me
around your little finger.

3.

Country girl, dark hair, 20,
naturally cute, due to accident
slight limp but it doesn't affect
the things I like to do. I am fun
to be with & still live
with my parents. I am seeking
a man who can understand
that I can't really run wild.

4.

Good old country boy
50s going on 40s
like to dine, dance
& cuddle with a good
old country girl with
tractor. Any age if
you are neat & trim.
please send picture
of tractor. I am
financially secure &
have a big barn for
tractor. Also have
swimming pool to enjoy
after chores are done.

5.

Queen-size Scorpio, shy
green eyes, speaks German, very fair
hair more salt than pepper.
I don't like feeling USDA
inspected in the singles bars
& there's more to life anyway
like sensuous clothing, backrubs,

rib-tickling by firelight, changing
careers not diapers. I sparkle
to nicknames. I've had my fill
of road lizards. I love longhair cats
& men. I'd like to meet a guy who is fun,
impulsive & original but also blends
when necessary. A big man with matching
sense of humor, maybe, to stimulate me.
Full-figured, dieting, love-plump—
in 30 lbs I'll be a fox.

    6.

Helicopter pilot raised right in Ohio
black hair green eyes good body
my main events are martial arts
& occult sciences. I like slow
dancing, some books, TV, VCR, CW
music. Steady job, good company,
recently re-singled. Just evil enough
to have loads of fun. Looking for same.
This is no game.

    7.

Our mom is looking for a guy
to have a great relationship with—
possibly lasting. Male model type
who loves to do things, also must
love kids & sad movies 'cause
she's very feminine & attractive,
30, divorced with two beautiful
little reproductions. My sister is 7
& I am a boy.

REARRANGING THINGS YOU SAID

You said you were only curious
breezing in on a whim and staying

You were confused by the order here
the memorial still of still life

*(Maybe he's dead or just resting
maybe he's just testing me)*

You paced the room rearranging things
books and carpets and blankets and stains

Pictures on the floor, cups against the wall
as though gravity made no sense here

(You said, *A strange thing in Mexico
happened to me on a trampoline)*

You paced the room rearranging things
like the light and the odor of the night

(You said, *You make my flower sweat
you said, You make my sweater wet)*

Drawing the thread of your being here
around the armchair where I sat, tongue

Tied in silk scarves of silence where
my parched skin waits for you to come back

Like wind on a burn, cool, searching
and drawn to the still open window

(You said, *Your eyes are greedy children
you said, Your mind is a wrinkled bed)*

You paced the room rearranging things
and now everything you touched is changed

(You said, *I can do anything I want
I can do anything I want to here*

Drip wax on your skin
trace fate in the fault lines of your hand

Be unreal, bitch, spill wine, dance, even state facts
this is the only place where everything

That has a place has no proper place
in fact, it's where I belong)

Curious pleasure, curious pain, too much:
change is everything you touch.

NAKED NOT NUDE

> *"When I'm painting people in clothes, I'm always thinking*
> *very much of naked people, or animals dressed."*
> —Lucian Freud

Memory is an ill-lit room
where nothing is discarded

An anteroom or attic where
detectives do their research

(Just the facts, please, ma'am
the unembarrassable facts)

And recycle what facts don't fit
today's cold case but just might

Tomorrow's. Under the gaslights
immune to her own tears, she tears up

Silk scarves she once wore as bandana tops
into gauze bandages. Married muses

Like her, of a certain age and wounded
are called by certain men *naked not nude.*

IS THAT A LANDSCAPE OUT MY WINDOW?

"The landscape is the woman, and there is
Woman in the Landscapes."
—Willem de Kooning

Is that a landscape out my window
is that a mirror in my bed

Are all our hopes an afterglow
of teen romance, a backlit silhouette

If I die before tomorrow morning
will you censor what I might have said

Is my skin just your dark shadow
negligee of hermaphroditic dread

Is that a graveyard out my window
my black widow still unwed

Is that a sandscape out our window
shifting dunes with battered hearts unbled

Is that soft arc of our horizon fading
all our unburied children dead

Am I seeing what I'm seeing
an owl protruding from my head

Downcast flaming cherub lodged between us
melting stained-glass dreams for lead

In some towering cell-phone steeple
censoring all that must be kept unsaid.

THIS DEGRADATION

I am a deer between cool sheets.
Drowsing owls, perched to look forward
and backward, sound the hours.

While you, minute by minute, you
with that tangle of charged wire
between your legs heat the bed;
while you, moment by moment, you,
your spine a necklace of broken pearls,
are missing. You, tailless and pale
hairless velvet toy of the chalk-white
teeth soft as whelks
who used to shrink from my kisses,
you were the cause of this incontinent
enchantment, this degradation.

No wonder I strike back
peel your skin away in strips
pulverize your precious spine
with my pretty shoes until
cool gland and arrogant flesh
are tender enough for my impeccable
palate. You always held your tongue
around me because you had no faith
in my intelligence, because you took the blame
on yourself, mouthing your round desire
like wind-blown foam on a salt-lick.

You realize, of course, quite naturally
that I understand these particulars
that you kept so secret inside
your zippered purse like instruments
of torture for the slow and angular progress
of your human martyrdom.

I shall keep you in a hair and velvet shell
under this froth of fresh linen
and break you hourly between the sheets.

THE MUSIC OF SNAPDRAGONS IS FRAGRANT

The disemboweled unicorn
laughs in a mad wood

Beech trees groan
for love of me

The sinecure of mulch
hugs my resistless worm

Times inch by inch
in my employ

Symmetry of waiting
concubine of suicide

Symmetry of waiting
feeds my decay

Waiters tip tea in a mango grove
I drive insects wild.

THE NOVELIST ON THE CARPET

To get at the truth I tried to stick
to facts, but everything was so slippery

I had to change my tactic. These erasures
opened up vistas I never knew existed

A new woman walked through the first razed door
beautiful, moody, her punk eyes wide, preoccupied

Barbaric exasperation, her cool Patti Smith
met my blank Richard Hell

Enclosed behind impenetrable pride
she ignored me: I was happy

I would be slim as a needle and slip through
the telescopic peep-hole in her third eye

To live alongside her thoughts in their muffled space
silent as a sliver of glass on the carpet

One day it's spring cleaning and I'm swept out
in a frenzy, to be found out in the sole of her

Foot: a bubble of blood wells up like an eye
winks at her, and gives my hiding place away.

CEUX-CI NE SONT PAS DES POÈMES D'AMOUR

These are not love poems
they are lead weights on a fishing line

These are not lines
they are highwires to leap from and die

These are not dies to be cast
they are living breaths spiraling into the depths

These are not deep
they are shallow feints, parries, and reverses

These are not verses
they are treaties meant to appease the mean-spirited

These are not pleas
they are arguments with our pleasures and ourselves

These are not pelf
they are payments down to the ringmaster

These are not faster
they are a slower means to a glowing end

These are not sent
they are received by one eternally deceived

These are not to be believed
they are the despair unspoken in unpublished books

These are not just good looks
they are telegrams tapped out by the freshly dead

These are not lead
they are hooks at the end of miles of fishing line

These are not wine
they are hearts savored on a skewer, with tequila, salt and lime.

TONIGHT THE VODKA TASTES LIKE CHOCOLATE

Timișoara

Tonight the vodka tastes like chocolate
a hunger that tastes like getting used to

It may take a week or a couple of country miles
it depends on what week and which country

A taxi is a taxi is a taxi
we take it as far as it will go

Trusting the driver as though
he were destiny

Thankful just to be away from home
like beat dogs out in the pouring rain

Twilight comes early in this time zone
bats circle the cathedral and bells drone

A country is not a thing we own
though we take it with us wherever we go

It owns us, like our dowager superego
holding us up by the collar or an ear

We think we're free of it while we're in its power
when we try to shake it it shakes us

Like a bride tangled up in her bridal train
like the handle of a suitcase that won't let go.

THE WOMAN AT THE PARTY WITH HER ENTOURAGE

> " . . . she was an ellipsis unto herself."
> —Ross Feld, *Guston in Time*

Wee, sleekit, with sensitive nostrils
the woman with the cluttered house
full of beautiful objects arrives

at the party with her entourage.
They give her courage
for any number of things,

to disparage
if not to dance, or to sing
a cynical note of praise.

She accepts a glass and compliments
on her dress.
Such a lovely party! And its echo:

Parties are such sweet sorrow.
The repartee is rich
with innuendo.

She's come, she says,
to say good-bye,
and she sniffs the wine.

It's cheap
and reminds her of former lives:
the fedora on Sunset Beach,

Puccini's mistress
nailed naked on the plowed sand
a rock in each elegant hand.

Wrinkles that crease her knuckles now
make her think of elbows
clad in elephant skin.

To think, her grip once choked
a violin. She grows a little wistful
in the house's emptiness

and longs for things she cannot name
but knows she has them stowed at home
somewhere. With her money

the future seems friendly
and her artist friends list affiliations
with galleries, churches, and corporations.

Foyers of the rich contain
the beautiful things they've done.
When someone asks how much they got

for this or that stained window
they tastefully decline
another glass of wine and get

down to the business of design.
*This wall for instance
could use a photographic distance,*

*a window on the world like mine
or one of his abstractions
I'd recommend*

*a dance in two dimensions
that never ends.*
They glide along the long hallway

like early morning shadows.
The artlessness offends
their sense of things.

The nakedness defends
itself too well against
them and their profession

based on taste and possession.
This interior, they say in unison,
I do not like it, like it is.

They offer up
their comments gratis.
How Spartan, says one, another,

Ascetic, a third through thinnest lips lisps
Why, your walls are
thimply nude!

In the corners of the blue room
mattress and chair sit modestly apart
while they discuss the facts of art

as though the room were furnished
for voyeurs instead of lovers.
Talking about *things* as though

they mattered, they forget
the only excuse for things:
to do away with the need for things.

Suddenly sad, she cloisters herself in the toilet
napkining her nostrils, remembering
the night she danced the Dumka

with sweet Tereza on the terrace
outside Paris. She wonders:
(The reason for things is what?

To remind us of beauty
we have not got?)
Then she promptly conjures up

the night she squeezed her breast
(Tereza's) and out came a blushing pearl
a lozenge to loll upon her tongue.

She feels a little faint now but not long
ago she had a brace of poets among
her beautiful objects read to her.

They put everything in their mouths
(including her) and left the house
(and her) in ruin.

In the mirror she makes up
excuses for her absence
just adjustments of the things

she's always been afraid she knows.
She casts a backward glance at that and goes
back to the farewell dance.

WHO LOVES THE FROG?

The princess is reading poetry
(She has nothing left to buy)
What she owns is what she knows
She rents palaces with her eye.

It's a backyard kind of meditation
a birdbath kind of musing
a ruffling of feathers in stale water
a way of warding off attacks of
boredom on a useless Sunday after
noon when only a hose and broom attract
the idle hand of the once-upon-attractive man
who is so easily sidetracked as he waters
the bloodshot roses that droop amid ageratum
and iris, his garden's agenesis interrupted
by a wayward-ever-after reminder of
the obvious question, gone possible, that pops
up like a bubble in the pond:
        Who loves the frog?

Now that the patio's spic-and-span he drops
into the low-slung hammock chewing
Velveeta with sweet pickles and Spam,
warm beer gurgling his gut. The rake's been put
away, hose rolled up, and blonde besom of
the old dance stowed, his tools shut up in shed.
He knows that he has had his day. Only
the birdbath trickles. He runs his palm
across his prickles. He needs to shave
before his wife comes home from her Methodist
matinee. Crispering leaves can have their say:
with her cryptic arrival the question
bobs up like a bottle from beyond:
        Who loves the frog?

BLATANCIES OF WHALEBONE

Blatancies of whalebone
and pirouettes of pig
are meaningless consistencies
that claim the stakes are big.

In children's lit where minds are made
and man falls short of Moby Dick,
pregnant pauses hide in clauses
and gods grow pale and sick.

Blatancies of whalebone
and pirouettes of pig
give rise to vague conspiracies
that blurt *the game is rigged!*

We come to think in our own way
what's *really* real isn't here and now
but weird like Virgin Mother's Day
or a dead father's clouded brow.

Blatancies of whalebone
and pirouettes of pig
make meaning-mongers apoplectic
especially the local prig.

So take this nonsense for what it is
and don't in dreams forget to dig
for blatancies of whalebone
and pirouettes of pig.

SHE CHANNELS HER LATE FATHER BY SHARING HIS RECORD COLLECTION ON TIKTOK

Her beauty is synaesthetic. One might even say Orphic. What is it, exactly? Is it her self-possession, a cool affectation that betrays no trace of giggle anywhere in her repertoire? Is it her appearance, the dark hair, soft, feathery, even when up, framing her strong features, the rounded square jaw, the firm soft lips, the triumphal arch of bangs cut halfway up her forehead to showcase signature brows (somehow immobile yet expressive) more entrancing than Frida Kahlo's, fanned over wide eyes straight out of a Fayum funerary mummy portrait, eyes that would look bored if they were not so at ease with what she sees (the musical eternity her father now inhabits) and with what sees her (us, her eavesdropping voyeurs) online? Or is it her sincerity, almost teary at times, a tracery of fine-line tattoos here and there suggesting a willingness to suffer for art? *Souffrir pour être belle,* yes. Or maybe it is just those all-important, indispensable ears, whether festooned with clip-on paste diamonds or pierced dangles (one envies the vintage stores where she shops), those ears that are one with what she hears and shares—the library of her late father's record collection—ears perfectly attuned to the invisible mystery, perfectly molded or inherited to hold the fluid weight of any genre of music, from pop-rock metal, folk-jazz-razzmatazz fusion, psychedelic croon, big band bassoon, to dying disco—ears like the handles on a Greek amphora, larger than life—ears striving upward like twin spires of a Gothic cathedral or the wings of the Sidney Opera House—not so large as to startle and yet voluminous. In fact . . .

Her formula is as fascinating as her digital persona. She begins by announcing another episode of sharing her late father's record collection with an album, "so what are we going to listen to today?" as she fingers a quick midair cat's cradle, head tilted, having picked a disc, famous or obscure, more or less (we assume) at random, then "let's give it a listen" for a lesson in sincere music appreciation. Turntable spins, a tiny horse or pig or pickle pirouettes in the center, while she half-reclines on the billowing bedclothes of her unmade bed, gazing into the distance beyond her pink bedroom, listening with those Coptic eyes, chin leading the rhythms in her head, side to side (costume quick-changes, almost imperceptible, from jeans and peasant blouse to a pink feather bolero half-jacket, cowboy hat and shades). Only her head obeys the music, led by elfin ears and the beauty mark on her left jawline. Her smooth neck flexes and swans along the ledge of her clavicle then back again, necklines modest, bodices of peasant cotton and linen, sometimes high fashion, sometimes old-fashioned, always eclectic. Bows and boas, and a T-shirt worn inside-out and backwards, tag at her throat proclaiming I ♥ NY. Her nails painted blood-red to match the heart or sparkles or jet black, tracing spidery patterns in the air as she makes her musicological points as naively as she can about "nice" melodies and "really cute" riffs, and "charming" phrasing.

She concludes by stretching catlike as her Persian cat on her Persian carpet, frayed album at her fingertips. asking in her best upspeak: "Have you listened to this albu-uh-m?" Then blows us a kiss from her fingertips as the warm finale (or finish, layered and complex, as a whisky critic might say) to conclude today's seance, a gift, her presentation of another specimen from her late father's record collection.

CANNIBAL AFFECTATIONS

I have adopted a Panama hat
like a sophisticated cannibal

Dandified in missionary spats
white skins with meat still clinging to fur

I wear it at my typewriter
inky ribbons for a hatband

The ragged brim raked at an angle
to cast an aesthetic elephant shadow over my work

All this is designed to reassure
her I would seduce, her I would reduce

To texture, and of course myself mirrored
in each lovely fissure of her weathered skin

My sense of fashion is stillborn
my sense of humanity, decor

My sense of humility, humor
a dark and twisted gnarled root, without a moral purpose

Like any conflict-loving Goth I treasure
my weapons as my art. Trophies dangle

Below my belt to remind me like ringing spurs
of all I've ever felt and all, thank gods, I've ceased to feel

I pretend to be oblivious to danger
and its difficult truths. I continue to harm

Myself if not others. Crushed by the shadow of her
I compose (in whisps and purrs) my gray memoirs.

VIRGIN BRIDES AND TENNIS PLAYERS

Corpses always dress in white
like virgin brides and tennis players

Oblivious to cheers and lamentation
at the celebration of their sacrifice

Uniforms to attract marauding stares
centers of attention but there's a catch

After the party after the wake
sudden isolation falls like a beaded curtain

Like pebbles on polished hollow oak
applause in the democratic bleachers

Unseen and unmolested they tear up towels
into squares of lacy gauze to mop up

Pools of hymen blood so thin and bright
so salinated with sweat and tears and loss

That an ad hoc loneliness ensues
courting the disaster of a quick divorce

Sportive stories of the future dead:
love, deuce, advantage, set, match.

APATHETIC PANTOUMERY

The ideal perspective is purely apathetic
so don't bother us with current events

Or religious sects like the Rosicrucians
we don't go in for political parties

It's not that we're unhappy with current events
in fact they tend to support our belief that it's stupid

To go around politicizing parties
especially when there are better things to do

Like going to the zoo if you want to see a bunch of stupid
asses and elephants and other party mammals

Who usually have better things to do
than trying to get invited to *people's* parties

Asses and elephants never talk to other species
(have you ever noticed? Isn't it sad?)

When they're at these hypocritical parties
that even we wouldn't be caught dead at

You've never noticed it, how sad?
then you've never sat next to a Rosicrucian

Even we wouldn't be caught dead at
one of *their* parties

You might have religious sex with a Rosicrucian
which might not be too bad

If you never again got invited to their parties
or had the ideal retrospective

Come to think of it, that too might not be too bad
but if you're no connoisseur of boredom it could be murder

Unless you have the surreal perspective
but only a prime minister is that apathetic

We nihilists of boredom, we're simply murder
so we don't get invited to a lot of church socials

With the wives of Rosicrucian ministers who are so pathetic
and dedicated to the art of the perfect sermon

Because we aren't often invited, people think we're antisocial
or snotty like we have something better to do

Than dedicate our wives to the perfect merman
which, when you think of it, isn't exactly true

But people who think we have nothing better to do
probably go door-to-door for political parties

Spreading rumors about us that just aren't true—
unless you take a certain perspective

But since we don't crash political parties
or talk safe sex with the Rosicrucian crew

Who's going to understand that we take a certain view?
It's true: the apathetic ideal is purely reflective.

THE SWEETNESS OF LIFE

Yesterday I was eating honey
and yoghurt on the balcony.
There was a bee balancing on the rim
of the honey jar, doing backbends.
With the book I was reading I beheaded him.
His head landed in the honey. Jaws kept
sucking, and antennae kept on waving.
These exertions kept his head afloat,
propelling it forward, like the masthead
of some allegorical boat.

Places

ANIMAL DEMONS, INCLUDING ONE
RESEMBLING A MAD SHINTO PRIEST,
CAROUSE ON AN ENORMOUS BOLT OF CLOTH.
A CLAWED MONSTER HIDES UNDERNEATH.

OFTEN I STOP IN MID-SENTENCE, RECALL

3420 Sansom Street

Often I stop in mid-sentence, recall
all those rented rooms, apartments, houses

That felt more like compartments on a train
burrowing into the night than home. This

Is the raw material, sketches of
vast interconnected hollows through which

A headless horseman gallops in search of
a place to lay his disembodied ears

Folded like an old pair of brakeman's gloves
bursting with music of the night. The foiled

Plot was to find some modest warren with
breathing room for two and furnished with a

Player piano. Instead we landed
real toads in a real garden, unlike that

Helmet in the courtyard in *Otranto*
in Walpole's Gothic wonderland, peopled

With monks, bleeding nuns, and a white puppy
like the one that cured Madame HPB

In a little stone house in Philly so
she might rise again theosophically

Find her legs again philosophically,
and carry on with her humbuggery.

HERE, HALFWAY

Here, halfway
running I spun round without stopping

Toward the room I had run from
back through the closeted halls I'd lit

Dimmer as I descended again
I found my first lights dead

Saw myself in a corner dying
and fled not wanting not able to help

Back to where I'd left myself
here, halfway

Running again gasping hoping to breathe a wind
beyond the threshold
to open the door.

FORTY AIN'T SO BAD

I've had worse toothaches
bigger corns on smaller toes
bet big on worse odds for smaller stakes
learned how and why not to pose.

I've written better poems than this
and sold them gladly for a kiss.
I've made worse beginnings, waged
better battles, suffered more tragic ends.

Still working on those middle things
like age and midriffs that keep getting fatter.
It doesn't matter, it's all just a stage.

Forty ain't so bad, considering
the alternative—now that I've quit
collecting wedding rings.

MACOMBER, FRANCIS AND HIS ELEGIAC DANCES

"Are you feeling better, Francis, my pearl?"
—Ernest Hemingway

The short happy life is longer by half
than the one we were expecting

This one always seems to go on too long
like a lecture, an opera, a birth, a bad dream

It's the repetition to which we object
don't you agree, Mr Wilson? We agree:

Like every professional who deals in deficits
I'm ready to collect my benefits

Why should I pretend I'm sorry
living my life like a guy on safari.

NIGHTWATCHMAN READS BECKETT ON PROUST

"To die fighting was the perfect antithesis of his
whole practice, faith, and intention."
—Samuel Beckett, *Murphy*

As night watchman on the graveyard shift
the aging student reads Beckett and writes about Time's

Trilogy—*perpetuum mobile* of all desire—
as Murphy plays chess with inmates at the asylum

Every hour at "unpredictable intervals" he lifts
his head to scan the lot, then makes his rounds among

Gray shipping containers in elephantine slumber
waiting for their drivers to whip them awake

His flashlight illuminates the opaque Oregon drizzle
Northwest coastal fog thickening toward an even obscurer

Ledge of dawn. Should he meet some thief or hijacker
in the mist, how, he wonders, would he greet them?

With a meek whistle and a shout, or a friendly bark
of mutual ambivalence about their respective jobs?

After all, he bears no grudge, much less arms
and their roles are as perfunctory as their pay

As night grows darker he looks forward to the coming day
and returns to the ill-lit ill-heated guard shack

Because he cares (above all) what Beckett has to say
curious what clever move Murphy has made behind his back

Because only in books does he find what he's looking for
sanity in the asylum, inmates who still get the rules of the game.

SLEEPLESS IN CUERNAVACA

Here in Cuernavaca my insomnia has become
unbearable, gored by the guilt of gold guitars

I vaguely remember dreaming that
Wolfsburg of Zaragoza was buried

To the tune of falling stars. I'm not troubled
by such visions but by these packs of wild dogs

That sniff and hump and bark (like we do
or pretend to) beneath the blue gazebo

Outside Cholula they say they're rebuilding
the pyramids, replacing the asylum at the base

With discos and mezcal bars. I can see it now
building blocks of smog and burning tar

And at the top will be the staring eye of my insomnia
speared on the horn of a mad guitar.

THE HAUNTING OF HOUSES

"If there is one thing innocence is not, it is a house."
—Thom Gunn

The haunting of houses has nothing to do
with the dead; has everything to do with those
door-down-kickers who arrive in the night
with affidavits for you to sign. You refuse to sign
and you refuse to sign until you decide to sign.

The haunting begins when you begin to see
Old Friends leaning dead drunk in doorways with
a drink in each hand thinking they know what
you think when they don't even know what you want
to drink, and you think: it's time for a change.

The haunting is here when you see Old Lovers
throwing off the last of their clothes for the first time
again and you forget what it was about their bodies
in the dark or their wronged faces in the yellow
bruise of morning that made you look away.

Then you recall: the haunting is in full swing
when they look good to you again, lying there
doubled up crying or crossing the room, proud
and unselfconscious as elephants crossing the road,
glimpsed and gone before you can unshoulder your gun and shoot.

The haunting begins to end when you sense
in the crowded ecosphere the human stench
of an exorcism, incense burning and a prayer
when no one else is there but you and the
ubiquitous presence of a gray immensity.

You have had enough of hangers-on, of friends
who have kissed your ass once too often or
your girlfriend in the kitchen once. Yet
the haunting goes on, long after dawn when you
kicked them out and closed your eyes to try to forget.

If only you could forget to forget. You see it all crystal
in retrospect, icepick in your palm, ice cubes on the sheets,
a woman parting her lips, a man falling through the table,
a spurt of blood, a girl giving up what she has to give,
and you for a second coming have no nostalgia, none.

It has come to an end when you pick yourself up
by falling in love with a person or a country
or an idea or when you are haunted by the thought
of leaving everything, all ideas of loyalty and love
behind, when you are making preparations.

MOVING DAY

The host and hostess are packing up their stratagems
in duffel bags, giving away what will have no value

Where they're going. They give away old souvenirs
books and records, a bicycle, a wool-silk tapestry

From Ouarzazate, dishes and old love letters, history
and astrology, topographical maps of deserts

Already navigated. The beautiful elephant saddle
they keep. We live here like we're camping in, we put

Nothing away for a soggy day. After all, we're not
chipmunks filling our cheeks with future fodder

Nor any kind of monks who genuflect for merit
nor hip nuns whose perpetual adoration is said to be

Its own reward. We're not trading in pasts or futures
not waiting for spot-like moments of domesticity

Recollected in tranquility. We've packed our present
into raku pots and smashed them in the bonfire of our insanities

Before stuffing the memorial ashes of our notoriety
into some reluctant someone's basement or attic

None of our friends or family consider our things worth
keeping. None of our furniture can be called unique

Why, it's not even vintage, much less antique
our reputation is scuffed and scarred, much in need

Of refurbishing, not unlike the dubious fame
of this old haunted house. Its history is no mystery

Every room in what we've never called home
is considered by some to be a den of iniquity

Ashes to ashes and dust to dust, it doesn't need us
to gussy it up. When all the glasses are broken and all

The wine is drunk, everything worth anything can fit
into one gray trunk. Would you like this fork? It's yours.

THE NEW BUCHAREST

It's not chaos, au contraire
so much ugliness can only have been planned

Chaos is a lot of things but ugly it's not.
Not always.

Chaos is dangerous, meaty, random, rundown, violent, upbeat,
      beat-up, silly, weird, American, damned, joyous, turned
      upside-down, inside-out and sprawling, crawling, purple,
      howling, hungry, satiable, insatiable, curious . . .
Chaos is furious, never canned, inimical to man
Chaos is never planned.

Wandering these darkened streets
      empty of bistros on every corner
seeing the nightlife—with all its dangers
      bad taste, discos, risks, whackos—
that isn't there, but could be,
      should be, should have been,
could have been, is, in absentia
      (all it has is a city dementia), then
I want a big stick of chaos in my hand
      to murder again the little man
who turned the Paris of Eastern Europe
      into a plan.
Once is enough: never again.

AN AMERICAN SOCIOLOGIST IN ROMANIA

"If I see one more Gypsy kid without feet
I'll scream. You notice their mothers
never whack off their hands, oh no!
Hands we let them keep.
Those dirty little fingers are tools of the trade
valuable as ivory, pretty as jade,
and necessary.

For pushing the little Porgie-board
For pulling up your skirt, plucking at your heels
For wiping the eternal rosary of snot
For exploring pockets, for imploring
(*I luff you, madam. Giff me a dolor!*)
For adding up at the end of the day
all the little weightless communion wafers,
cinci lei, cinci lei, cinci lei . . .

Coins in exchange for the phantom pain
(there goes one now, down the stairs on his stumps
into the underground. Shall we take the escalator?
Never mind that, we'll give him something later)
the day's gain."

THE MOVING VANS MARKED METAPHOR

Mytilene

On Lesbos the moving vans line up on the wharf
a chorus line of elephants tied trunk-to-tail

Swaying along the *limani,* nudging each other
up the ramps into the bowels of the boat

Bound for Samos, each one marked ΜΕΤΑΦΟΡΕΣ
and vanish. They bear the weight of everything

The gypsies cannot bear to leave behind
on deck the drivers step over the sleeping

Family wrapped in blankets and drink
thick sweet coffee *metrio, parakalo!*

And sit near a window dozing to the dazzle
of sun on the wave, to the drizzle of blood

In their veins, and to the vibration coming
up from the hold, a sad exotic roar

And deafening odor of elephant
metaphor as the ferry leaves the harbor

Under the boat the dolphins sing
in the silver-blue Aegean

The drivers' spoons clink worriedly
over their cargo. The gypsies stir

In their bittersweet coffee sleep and snore
the elephants begin to dance.

THINGS WE NOTICED IN THE TAVERNA

Skopelos

Two men stroking their chins
one man laughing under his hat

Five men taking a drink, simultaneously
one man sitting thoughtfully, smoking

Three men listening to each other
two men sucking their teeth

Four men all ears
one man going outside

Three men coming in
one man singing to himself

One man taking orders
five men with their arms in the air

One man sitting thoughtfully, not smoking
one woman entering

Thirteen men distracted
one man stroking his chin

Two men laughing outright under their hats
one woman going outside

One man sucking his teeth
two men taking a drink, simultaneously

Two men going out
one man sitting thoughtfully, doing nothing

Two men stroking their chins
one man coming in.

THE WAITER

Hey you, the anorexic girl at the blue tin table
white cup and saucer white as bone at your wrist

Red as Santorini sand! What do you think of the empty
caves in the cliffs where Nazis stockpiled ammunition

And how do you feel about nuclear fission?
what are you doing drinking coffee all morning long

Sifting sunlight through your loose-fitting anonymity
letting the wind get intimate with you

And why do you use so much sugar? Why not take a swim
in the cellophane bay or pick up a tourist or his wife for the day

Instead of choking down that endless chain of cigarettes
coffee, ouzo, and novels? Why inch your chair away

Along the embankment postcard picturesque and so
precipitous and finish a glass and give a finger-snap

For your waiter and why do you drink so much water?
this is not some melancholy subtitled foreign movie

Romantic farce for the spiritually anemic ending
in an atmospheric drowning or death dance

Oh, but I bet you think you're the star! Of course, who's to say
what's best for you, not I. So look my way, call your waiter

For more coffee and water, I dare you, after all
that's what I'm here for, your voyeur. And what would you do

If I said don't go after you've paid your bill, or made you stay
until the sun sets safely behind the hill?

DREAMING OF EUCALYPTUS

Send me a postcard when you get there
Give me a ring when you get back.

Come spring we'll get away from all this
and find some old island of sun and rock

In the loose weave of a hammock breeze
until we feel summer embalming us
        and dream of eucalyptus

You'll be fragrant as a peach split by the sun
I'll be pale shade for black island sand

Stripped of our secrets and calm pretenses
we'll dive deep and startle the Cycladean sea
        and dream of eucalyptus

Because you love the full moon
God would screw in a new lightbulb every night

Learn to speak Greek again, give up
modern ethics for ancient aesthetics
        and dream of eucalyptus

Promise me never to forget yourself again
or the days when you were my next of sin

I'll remind myself you can never be mine
and rebody myself from time to time
        and dream only of you.

SAPPHO'S ELEPHANT

Lately I sit at my middle-aged table
patch phrases of childishly broken Greek

A tongue I could never hope to speak
learning by rote what burning Sappho

Spontaneously sung as the ceiling fan
kisses my cheek. Sappho's elephant was Eros

He battered her portals of ivory and horn:
Epithalamia and Eleutheria

A girl's thick scent transported her
a girl's thick ankles crushed her

She wrapped her legs around his purple
saddle and let herself be carried

Over the humpback island. Later, a Cretan
ballerina hung on his low-slung coral tusk

To be kissed by the poet's song
drunk on a girl's breath swollen with dusk

Her favorite season was while hunting
elephants mad with musth.

INTERREGNUM: OR THE STONE OPERATION

Meester snyt die keye ras
Myne name is Lubbert das.
—Hieronymus Bosch, *The Stone Operation*

She sat singing on her father's stone
thinking it was her father's throne
and scolded the old caretaker who
had come to sit near saying:
"The fools, the curs, the gelded badgers!
They bury the bones of their dead
only to dig them up again.
The fools, the curs, the gelded badgers!
But O that I might kiss his knuckles again."
To which the caretaker pinkly replied:
"Tooth buried inna pilla
disappears inna murnin."

   1. Madrid

Watching them enact the grisly script
in the gold and black design
she stands in the Prado perplexed . . .

   2. 's-Hertogenbosch

Bemused, a nun, chin in hand,
leans pondering perhaps
the plight of the theologian.
Or wondering perhaps
how Erasmus could condone
what Brant before him
found malign. (The latter of whom
merely hadn't the spunk
to sit on his ire.) There's the monk,
there the surgeon, there the patient
fool who, plump and compliant,

awaits the cure. Soon the bloody tulip
will lie limp on the table.

   3. Basel

Zwingli of Zurich
and Luther of Leipzig
eruditely essayed to sink
Sebastian's fliggen blather.

Meanwhile, *affe!*
Christopher in Hispaniola
cavorted with naked island men
whereof no mortal ever knew.

But the hot pontoons kept afloat
and Martin after Wittenberg
kept his fine filibuster up
till Wurms dealt his fiasco.

(The sight of Martin on the run
toward the hamlet of Wartburg
proved too much for poor Sebastian
who within the week expired.)

   4. Rome

Pico della Mirandola sent up andante
a word of praise which eight years later
still had not reached Flanders.
               (Some say
Wimpfeling ate it on the way.)
            ("Damn the rotter,"
Gerhard groaned. "I wanted to hear
what that *ragazzo* had to say!"

5. *Paris*

She stands at the window.
Outside, coffees and cognac pour
in cafes. The amber sky blackens.
Eyes glisten.
The darkness is her mercury.
She bites the corners of her lips
and shifts to feel her slip crackle.
The brush is full of electricity—
or is it her hair,
or the air?

6. *California, Again*

On to logical issues!
But be it. *Narr!*
Be two bloody lips
the bulbs of which
(though your green fountain
twitch and spurt)
remain rooted in the ground.

Hie, Digger, and alas!
Yorick's hull is shucked.

7. *Le Jardin du cimetière*

      Back home, for her,
the caretaker sketches round faces in the dirt
with long-purples and serapia stones
and wipes his fingers on his shirt.

HOLLYWOOD

" . . . the one authentic rectum of civilization."
—H. L. Mencken

If only it were true what Antonioni said,
"Hollywood is like being nowhere
and talking to nobody about nothing."

That would have been interesting; a Zen koan,
instead of just an annoying collaborative investment,
a colorful, fashionable so-forth-and-so-on.

Disgraces

SEVERAL MONSTERS, CONTINUE THE
PROCESSION, INCLUDING ONE WITH A BUDDHIST
MONK'S ALMS BOWL ON ITS HEAD.

THANKS, IT'S GOOD FRIDAY IN FAIRFAX COUNTY

1.

In the new version Christ is nailed
to two planks of particleboard
on a Friday afternoon at Happy Hour.

Everybody trilling TGIF forgets
about the poor guy until it rains
then wonders how and why he got away

The makeshift cross crumbling by Sunday
into aspirin for the masses.

2.

Then comes a boy with cherry pit stains
on his jeans and the palms of his hands
a face like a dollar bill.

He lays claim to the truth of fiction that will
wash tons of sins away but can't conceal
the hatchet dripping native juices

A genocide of apples and cranberries, peaches
and the rape of one virgin black cherry tree.

NOVEMBER 2024

Then one day someone up and steals the furniture from your porch
you're annoyed but you think, *maybe they need it more than I do*

Only to find out they have plenty of furniture of their own
and plenty of porches to put it on, many more than you

In fact they are billionaires with houses and towers galore
they just don't want you to have what you need or to be at ease

Because it doesn't serve their purpose; only your primal fear
of losing what little you've got to those with even less than you

Will cause you to come begging to them to fix it with an X
twisted crucifix, crypto swastika, built from the bones of a little blue bird

When you wake up and complain that they've taken your porch
they turn around and claim that it's you who have stolen it from them

Now they are chipping away at the foundation of your house
and you think, *maybe I'll move to Canada, maybe I'll revolt*

But you know that you'll do nothing of the sort because anger
and greed and ignorance are universal, fear is eternal

And you are outnumbered. And you love your country. And you recall
what it was like to nap like the dead on what was once your porch.

JANUARY 2026

Crossing the Rainbow Bridge to Canada,
it's a bumpy ride over the dry Niagara,
only a trickle of red from the wound below,

flags flying overhead, the Maple Leaf
at half-staff on one side, twin U.S. banners
on the other: Stars and Stripes, and the McDonald's
Arch redacted to add the eight stolen
Venezuelan stars in cheap gold leaf
from Home Depot.
    And the quickly setting sun:
a leering orange troll with an oily glow
screaming like nails on a virtual chalkboard,
    "GREENLAND UBER ALLES!"

DA WABBIT WACE

—for Chris Champagne

Like dogs sidetracked by a real wabbit,
just when we begin to hit our stride
we move on to another race—
or so we think for that's a myth
a comfort zone, a bone we throw
to ourselves to keep our bark afloat
and our tail behind us, for anything
else is literally preposterous.
        The impossible that we avow keeps us
        anchored above the unfathomable now.

BUGS BUNNY, POSTMODERN POSTMORTEM

One day you find a bloody rabbit's foot
some toes still attached. Didn't Bugs Bunny

Have some pun or standing joke on that
and the nature of art? How cartoonists

Play with their characters' luck with a slip
of the pen or eraser? Bugs was both

A postmodernist and an animal
rights activist of tragicomic stature

Comfortable with the operatic
notion of the artist who plays havoc

With motion. A cynic who could think
on his feet, willing to weep, wail, cajole

Or dissemble for the Cause, either to keep
on his toes, or his toes on his paws, his nose

Clean and his claws to, a law unto, himself
Elmer Fudd was something else: a hunter

Homebody, redneck baby, nobody's son
everybody's pappy armed with a pop gun.

HYPOTHESIS WITH LITTLE SYMBOLISM AND LESS SCIENCE

*Abstract: As traditional fare for
target practice apples have no peers.*

Long before William Tell leveled his crossbow
fathers bedeviled sons with tough love
by chucking spears at their heads

or just above to pierce their halos.
Call it primal jealousy, Oedipus in reverse;
call it politics, folklore, religion, perverse.

It's only natural. From Adam to Abraham
whose fear and trembling were not for Isaac alone
but for all fathers and sons and fruits of the earth.

Take Newton, for instance, idling under branches.
Dull, pedantic, patriarchal Gravity got
his attention by aiming rotten apples at

his head and, taking no chances, dropped them
stem by stem, like any brute predictable father
teaching his insouciant son a lesson, about

gravitas no doubt, from the negligible altitude
of apple-tree limbs. Science tells us, too,
that if apples are not to be had one can take

aim at the earth with pears or spears in a pinch
and seldom miss. But tradition dictates
that there are no peers in target practice

for apples. We know too, from our own good sense
that apples unarrowed by symbols (much less
science) make better targets than weapons.

STILL LIFE WITH WAR

All those Renaissance skulls and rotten apples
don't fool me. Death and decay, disintegration,
are ripenings, food for thought, digestion.

We live in the autumn of autumns,
late in the day, when the old tribes find it
easy to justify anything, even murder

collateral damage the mere
drowning of superfluous kittens.
Every generation loves its genocide.

We open wide our bleeding mouths
like Bacon's Popes to scream because
even the victorious can claim to be victims

so long as they scream louder than their prey
who sit like a bowl of fresh fruit on a table,
mute, consumable, to be bitten with humility.

So don't tell me about aesthetic perspective.
Don't claim two dimensions to every story.
Let's face it: our shadows stalk us.

We may not think we like to kill,
but it's what we all believe in,
more than life, still.

STUDY FOR A MASSACRE OF THE INNOCENTS

Nothing is either good or bad but shooting makes it so.

Christ clings to his cross
Deplorables to their guns
Extremists to their slogans
Escapists to their fun
Talking heads to video rostrums
Simple minds to podcast pulpits
Killers to the Constitution
Everyone to the news:
Another shooting, a few boohoos.

Our logarithms make it so,
not thoughts and prayers,
only the action of our inaction.
We loop and loop and loop
pray and pray and pray away
pray away the gay
pray away the gray
pray away the bills we have to pay.

Our phones foam for attention
like rabid dogs nipping at our fingernails;
dyspeptic babies regurgitate
viral clouds of glory
to get their words' worth. We stroke
screens with epileptic thumbs. We scroll
echoed nostrums of religion—creation, sin,
sacrifice (oh so forsaken forgiveness), rebirth,
resurrection, retribution, revelation—to rectify
an original erratum we only hope to live to long enough
(forever) live up to, pretending it all was intentional,
part of the plan, as though it were what was meant
all along, a divine meme:
The good die young.

The trigger goes click click clickbait because
(the better the story, the bigger the headline)
the more innocent the target,
the sweeter the blood.

WATCHING SNOW FALL IN UKRAINE

—after Du Fu

The battle not yet over, fresh ghosts appear
this old man frets and grieves for strangers

Dying on the battleline of dubious borders
frayed clouds hang like laundry on the horizon

Snow dervishes whirl in the wind
pitchers overturned, cups empty

Firepits yet glow with undying embers
news breaks from afar; I sit up like a shot

But cannot bear to read the empty pages
of an old Russian book.

OBSESSED WITH THE NEWS AT BREAKFAST

The sun is up, promising a good day:
coffee hot, toast buttered, and fresh fruit
spread out on the newspaper.

But every time I gaze into the navel
of my orange I see the anus-mouth of a man
they call the president staring back at me.

I take the sharpest knife I own and slash
and slice and bite, but the flesh is rotten
inside and out, the juice bitter.

Another breakfast poisoned by newsprint,
what they like to call reality. The old joke:
black and white and re(a)d all over.

WHY MY CAT IS NAMED HITLER

—for J. T.

"I was at Kinko's today and I was surrounded
by a nauseating sea of cuteness, girls
with alligator things in their hair, buns up
here and a Bam-Bam thing over there and
Are you in such-and-such a class, too?
It makes me puke. And the boys are cute,
too. I mean, whatever happened to real men
with long hair and stinky armpits?

Cuteness: right up there with cats and fascists.

I don't want to know what my cat's name is,
don't tell me. I don't want to know. I know
already. It's Hitler: she signs treaties then attacks.
I don't want to hear that she has some cute name
like Cynthia. She's Hitler, like all cats.
Little black shirts, little brown shirts,
little calico shirts, they all have a cute little
swastika on their upraised right front leg."

I WANT TO WRITE A POEM THAT RHYMES JESUS

I was Philip Guston
looking at my ashtray
for inspiration—
and I could swear
there was a poem in there.

I want to write a poem that rhymes Jesus
with sneezes.

I want to write a poem that breathses
not one that wheezes.

I'll dedicate it to Tina Louises
and write it in kanji in Japaneses.

I don't want to write a poem that rhymes Buddha
with gouda. (It doesn't!) *Cheeses!*

A love poem maybe with hugs and squeezes
in spring or summer breezes,

Erotic with lots of birds and beeses
showing some poiesis expertises.

A drinking poem dedicated to Dionysus
like those revelries on skyphoi and marble friezes.

I'd even be happy to write about diseases
ones we share with our kinfolk rhesus

March against war and chant for peace, yes
even though ICE might try and seize us.

I'm down on my kneeses, Jesus, pleases,
forgive us our egregious catachreses.

SOMETIMES SOMETIMES IS NOW

sometimes I sit
like fluid in a cup
like sap in a tree
other times not

sometimes a human hand
can cleanse a conscience
more thoroughly than
a vacuum or a viaticum

sometimes a rental van
full of masked men
making fifty grand
is more dangerous than
a South American coup

sometimes Jesus is just
an excuse to turn
water into whining
and crude into coin

sometimes a book
bible or constitution
is just an empty cover
to justify the unjust

sometimes a lie becomes
a truth
masquerading
as Truth

sometimes I never feel so
tolerant or friendly or free
as when I am alone, empty
and the cup is me.

SOMETIMES OUR HUMAN

      sometimes
      our human
      fingernails
do a better job of scraping
burnt flesh from the ovens
pulling nails from our feet
      than a spade
      a subpoena
      or swastika
      in the shape
      of a crucifix
      crescent star
      or menorah
         *

      sometimes

JERUSALEM SYNDROME

*The best way to help, say the doctors at Kfar Shaul clinic,
is to get the patients out of the city and to their families.*

In Jerusalem the worship never stops.
The rain rains on the Dome of the Rock
and worship never stops.

We pray, write postcards, argue, shop
worship never stops.
Everything is holy, see, and worship never stops.

Backpackers preach, thou shalt not pay more
than so many dinar a day for a room, falafel and hummus
(ten shekels tops). Worship never stops.

They have seen the Promised Land, Thailand, Fiji
and every island in between, and have learned
a thing or two about currencies and mini-taxis.

In the Arab quarter all the signs are missing
all the omens point one way, through the maze
of all religions. Worship. Worship. Never stops.

Just a quick detour through Jericho, where it's 1417 CE
and we're all amazed. What to do differently?
Are we coming back? Preseeing questions of the day

Never mind that the Prime Minister wants funds
for the residence decor. Never mind that hundreds
died today in a quake in northern Iran.

Never mind that Netanyahu still fancies a future
with Lego cities in Gaza. This is not even news anymore.
Can you direct me to the Armenian quarter?

Follow the trail of blood and tears. I'm the Messiah
glad to meet you. Can you direct me to the Hotel Gloria
via the Dung Gate and genocide?

Not a chance. Jaffa! Jaffa! Tourist Information Center.
What do you think I am? Who do I think I am?
Oh no, am I suffering from Jerusalem syndrome?

Have I died and gone to heaven yet? It's . . .
smaller than I thought it would be and filthy
with religion and styrofoam cups.

Leave your shoes and women at the door
nine dollars US entrance to the Dome of the Rock
where the worship never stops.

How do we get to the Western Wall?
Follow the railing until you get to the wailing
there are two ways, but here you cannot pray

The tourist gate is there and there and there
look for the metal detectors and IDF soldiers
salute them, okay, but here one cannot pray.

Why worry all day? It's okay. Worry is a form of prayer
a circle of beads or a crown of thorns, wear them
at your own risk, though, or even the black halo

Commemorating the loss of Cordova to the Cross
wear them and weep. The worship never stops
worship never takes a holiday.

You've come to the Church of the Holy Sepulchre
where the black monk squats on an ottoman
clutching his breviary and evil-eyeing the tourists

And dreaming of Christ as Charlie Parker or Billie
Holliday and spikes of pure gold on the roof.
Leaving so soon? Don't forget the good book

You bought on the street. Or did you decide on the Torah chimes
instead? Maybe the video slideshow narrative display.
Now do you know the way? Souvenir worship never stops.

Catch a taxi at Damascus Gate from the West Bank to Jordan
across the bridge (thirty meters only), exit fee thirty dollars each
for a leap of faith. Cash only please. Your Visa is no good here.

For less than 666 shekels (200 dollars at the current rate about)
at the Gloria Hotel in Old Jerusalem you can stay and stay and
stay pray and pray and pray your sins away.

But then you must leave for Amman. Amman, amen,
where the worship also never stops, here in the land of the holy.
Which one is yours? Is that your wife? Stamps, this way please.

THE RUDE OLD GUY AT THE U-HAUL DROP-OFF IN BOULDER

Things ain't the way they used to be.
Things ain't fixed to satisfy me.

Miles and miles of new highways,
new taxes, tolls and HOV lanes nobody pays

attention to, certainly not me.
This ain't the country it used to be.

New construction goin' up like weeds,
condos for college kids and rich retirees.

Hikers, bikers, climbers, and some new breed
called "influencers" ain't the fluence we need.

May all their itty bits get caught in their spokes.
I pray that Bernie Sanders up and croaks.

Climate crisis, my ass, no EV for me,
a Hummer or my gas F-150.

Linen is the new denim, I heard it said,
faggot French casquettes for their pointy heads.

Parasites from blue cities swarming here
with wickable hoodies and underwear,

knocking off our squirrels, prairie dogs, and deer.
I can't keep up, is it "gay" now or "queer"?

This pandemic of pronouns and made-up names,
I wouldn't boohoo to see it all in flames.

These libtards with pockets packed with apps
Eye phones and Ear Pods, rechargeable backpacks.

Well, *we* don't take no digital IDs,
no public restrooms for morphodite peepees.

We don't Snapshat, DM, IG, or Zoom,
don't need no Nostradamus to know we're doomed.

We don't Snapshat, DM, IG, or Zoom,
don't need no Nostradamus to know we're doomed.

You want to know what'd make me grin?
All this lot deported to Oregon.

Better yet their heads bobbing in baskets,
Mexicans and their kids in caskets.

They can burn the flag and Ten Commandments
long as I keep my Second Amendments.

I hear they're puttin' up a brand new mall,
to hell with that! Build the goddamn Wall!

One big conflagration will do, a clean one-two,
every immigrant, Democrat and Jew.

Take the Catholics too, I don't give a screw
if it takes me too—so long as it burns all o' you.

POSTHUMANIST PROTAGORAS

"Theology after breakfast sticks to the eye."
—Wallace Stevens, "Les Plus Belles Pages"

Let's set Leonardo's Vitruvian Man aside
just for a moment and disregard the supposed

Measure of all things
failed steward, fouler of his own nest

Like a doll that has seen its day
and been put away

Until another gender or generation takes it up again
puts it on a new stage to replay

The epic hero who lost his head
the Renaissance hero whose father's dead

The Enlightenment's Dilettanti who lost their reason
the Romantic individualist who did himself in

The angst-ridden Existentialist smoking pipes in his den
and so on . . . Nothing exists in itself

Not even inmates, ingrates, and animals at the zoo
although we act like we do—exist, that is

Because according to Leonardo
a square peg *does* fit a round hole

Man like a starfish eats the world through his belly
and philosophizes, glib Scarecrow, to digest his roles

Navel-gazing as though this lint-pit were
compass axis and cosmic center

Instead of just another boxing ring of nerves
a monstrous mouth

With five arms that can regenerate themselves
when lopped or cropped

Just another *coup de dés*
that will never abolish chance.

PARADE OF ONCE WELL-REGARDED DEMONS

*—after Kawanable Kyōsai's Night Parade
of One Hundred Demons*

Like Aobōzu who always wants more children
Like the water Kappa that who taunts them
Like Nuribotoke who haunts them

Well-dressed demons of sick delight
Leak not all at once but dribble
Hideous livestreams come to light

Zombie buddhas in Wall Street suits
Sad diplomats in party hats
Dancing clueless new spy recruits

Protected (but not very well)
By weak-kneed laws and lawyers that
Should be sending them all to hell

Their names and faces all blacked out
While victims remain stripped naked
By rich men's cash and political clout

Aobōzu's one eye that hunts stray children
Nuribotoke's gray eyeballs that dangle
Kappa's cynical voyeuristic grin

Prey on vulnerable teens and tweens,
Grooming and zooming and dooming
Girls down and out and without means

To futures of guilt and self-harm
Impossible to exorcize
Possessed by self-hatred and money's charm

These *yōkai* climb into our heads
Defiant in denying crimes
With each news clip that feeds our dreads

Tongues lolling, eyes falling, grinning
They creep through altar doors ajar
Sick with sinning, slick with winning.

Aobōzus guised as wise factota
Prince Nuribotoke's sweaty stare
Dangling like an old man's scrota.

Yōkai are not what we need beware of
But powerful men and women who prey
On the future we need to take care of.

May the red dawn justice unmask
The everyday demons around us
And give them hell, that's all we ask.

Traces

*A DRAGON CHASES DEMONS, INCLUDING
A WINGED HAG, AT RIGHT, WHO IS
EMBRACING A TINY CREATURE. BELOW, A
ONE-EYED MONSTER WEARS A GRASS SKIRT.*

SPITTING IMAGES

*"But I am not a Buddhist—even that is denied me.
My spirit needs <u>matter</u>—a <u>medium</u>—which resists the
peaceful [. . .] Unlike a monk, my self or mind-self is
not my medium—I cannot contemplate myself <u>into</u> myself."*
—Philip Guston in a letter to Ross Feld, September 1978

The golden profile of that boulder:
A lion facing the rising sun.

Like a rube in the Uffizi
I wander through the abstract canvases
of nature offering my glosses, my impressions,
turning raw beauties into mere familiarities;
or worse, like a critic offering mere philosophies,
reversing the course of art.

There's Aunt Sally in that tree trunk
upside down, head buried in the ground,
her spindly legs splayed to the sky.

Or the Monkey King imprisoned
in that cliff-face for kalpas
grinning against the rain
with charm and mischief.

Didn't Michaelangelo claim that he was just
releasing forms trapped in adamantine?
Or was that Rodin?

I can hear Ruskin and Rothko tut-tutting
my pathetic infractions. Still,
I can't get over it—those spitting images:
that lion's gray-green mane gilded in the morning sun,
Monkey's inane petrotechnics, provocative and protective,
the dark mossy bark in the crotch of Aunt Sally's hemlock thighs.

I come back to Guston's late boots and cigarettes,
and his bulbous horizontal congregations
with light bulbs flipping us on and off:
tragic cartoons for the chaos
of our chunky lives.

IDIOSYNCRATIC ICONS: A MANIFESTO

—or maybe just a reading list

Andy Warhol's *Invisible Sculpture*
hits the mark on its invisible nose

Gertrude Stein's inimitable syntax
cuts to the bone of the risible rose

Ronald Firbank's coy eccentricities
reveal more than just one cardinal's pose

Mina Loy's lunatic baedekers map
terrains of futuristic furbelows

Georges Bataille's jaded girls and slim boyos
fixate on bulls' eyes and are led by the hose

Sappho's prolific infidelities
still echo on the island of Lesbos

Boccaccio's ten days of tales within tales
survived plagues of bluenoses and buboes

Balthus's impervious impure maidens
have done away with flirty underclothes

Nina Hamnett's tragic bohemian end
on a fence meant no more laughing torsos

Aubrey Beardsley's horny unicorn
taught Venus what to do with her elbows

Leonora Carrington's Mexican asylum
is where no one wants to but everyone soon goes

Freud's (Lucian's not Sigmund's) analyses
flay our complexes from ego to toes

And John Cage's famous emptinesses
spring the latch to set free our wingless woes

These are artists that speak to me more than
Leonardos or Michaelangelos

What we need are more Zazies in more Metros
more Raymond Queneaus—and more Oulipos.

CAUTIONARY SONG

—for Isabel

Isadora Duncan was a dancing fool;
She danced underwater in the swimming pool.
An Amilcar she drove in a long silk scarf
Till it caught in a wheel and her head popped

off!

THE ELEPHANT MEMORY

Istanbul

The elephant memory cuts a fine swath
through all our bullshit facticity with its

Literal and bulky hulking unoriginality
saddle her up, we'll take a ride on the towpath

Of sidelined data. What matter if we crush a few
withered morning glories on the vine?

Like the good Nasreddin Hodja on his donkey
assbackwards we'll ride bravely into past perfect

To humorless pedestrian lookie-loos who've lost
their sense of rumor we'll tip burnooses and raise

Sunglasses. Who'll mock our trumpeting metaphors
(a stately van of vehicles with no tenors) to them

We'll display lèse-majesté and toward the grave
skedaddle, wise to have kept our elephant saddle

And lucky not to have lost our taste for the tragicomic
detail, or cocktails spiked with shots of paradox

And drama, whatever gave our life delectation
without a destination. This, we suspect, is the only

Sacred text, our life, its tint and texture, a hint
of drunken reverence for its hallowed fumes

This, we believe, is what will be exhumed of us
when all is said and done

When we can't quite gallop off the edge of being
into kingdom come.

REPETITION IS AN ELEPHANT

—for Devorah Salazar

Repetition is relevant, she said, a habit
performed since childhood. Like gossip

Variations on a theme, creatively inconsistent
harmless as geometry to a ballerina

First the theorems, then their corollaries
first the fine arteries, then we put on our

Thinking capillaries. It's fun. It doesn't have to be
drudgery. Think of circus elephants learning to plié

Tricks to earn their keep at a trunk's length and hip-
to-hip on tippy-toe to prestissimo hip-hop ballet

First they learn to concentrate while clowns carouse
to Kachiturian, then adroitly to compose themselves

True ladies in mortarboards with tutus roomy enough
to house the homeless, laying it on thick

Biographers of the famous on fifty-gallon drums and
Katie the Elephant pole-dances to canned Chopin

All graduates will graduate again today—so they say
—and after the ceremony drink tea and gossip

Repetition is relevant, she said to herself, and then
she said it aloud: *Repetition is an elephant.*

JUBILATE ELEPHANTI

—with apologies to Christopher Smart and all cats,
living or dead, including Jules and Jim (1990–1992)

A pair of black cats dance a Smartass Minuet
atop a Saturday of manuscripts

These are our mostly silent roommates
one, not quite so Smart, jumps off houses

That's Jules, the one with the endearing limp, now known as
Mr. Crooked Whippy Tail after the accident

The other, his brother, goes by the name of Jim
doesn't fancy baths but likes to swim

We would have named them Roché and Duchamp
but settled for their novelistic avatars. Like them

Both ladies men, although sometimes in their quickness
they give up the hunt and hump one another

For they are a mixture of gravity and waggery
blessed in the artfulness of their movements

They both run out in traffic, though we live downtown
don't always come back quickly or in one piece

For they are fearless in the face of nine endings
for life is not teleological nor tautological to them

Their ears are perked, they're sly. They know what's what
and why nor to say so in no uncertain terms are they too shy

For their tongues are exceedingly pure though lacking in music
for they are at almighty play in all things Cosmic

For there is nothing brisker than a feline in motion
for they are more precious than Jewels and Gemstones

For the Electrical Fire is the Spiritual Substance
for they have the grace of lightfoot Elephants in Black Furs

That is to say—and I add nothing new here, just facts
none that you don't already know—they are Cats.

SMALL TOWN CLASSIFIED

I received word
that my peacock was walking
down Stagecoach Road.

Unfortunately, I was
in Chattanooga.

I just got back and
Marc, the peacock,
is not in his tree.

If anyone should see him tomorrow,
would you please shoot
me a text?

THE GUY WHO NOW READS
ONLY *FINNEGANS WAKE*

He is one of those people so averse
to change that he tries not to finish
reading a novel for fear of veering off
into unfamiliar territories of the
imagination. Thus he lingered in
the land of Proust like Moses in the desert
for decades until he discovered Joyce.
Having come to the end of lost time
four times, he made time to hang out with
Stephen D. and wandered with Leopold B.
through the streets of Dublin for many a
groundhog day of sixteen June, 1904
up to the very hour of beddy-bye,
procrastinating shamelessly with
sleepless Molly until he could no
longer put off the climax of her
breathless *yes yes yes* . . . But no,
there was another tome at hand, one
which many are called to begin but few
chosen to end, a world of language
with finesse without finis, forever and
ever, amen; one that promised to take him in
new directions to the very terminus of
his—in fact everyone's—imaginarium.
With great trepidation he took the book up,
cracked first his plump knuckles and then its
stately buckram spine and dove in . . . *riverrun,*
past Eve and Adam's . . . but soon he knew that
he would never have to worry about starting,
much less finishing another novel
because this one would suffice not only for
this life but also for the one to come,

changing thus once and for all the indirection
of his inner life, exhausting the weakening
wakening of words by a *commodius*
vicus of recirculation back by Eve and
Adam's environs to again begin
again, the end of the neverending end.

THE GIRL ON THE SWING IN THE CASINO

Even if we really see *just once* her
red hair shining like shredded new pennies

Freckles like nickels and FDR dimes
at the bottom of a faux-Roman fountain

It doesn't mean our hopes are drowned, on the
contrary: they leap like carp from boiling water

They rattle like jackpots raining lucre
or hope in the form of melon-sized desert hail

Instead of waiting for something momentous
for some sudden ghost ship to come into harbor

We can say we have loved if not wisely, timidly
from afar, but yes, we can say we have lived.

RICTUS SARDONICUS PLAYS SOLITAIRE IN THE DARK

The hemlock water dropwort is said in Homer's time to have
been fed to the elderly when they could no longer support
themselves, leaving a sardonic smile on the face of the corpse.

Playing solitaire was an open sesame, a key
to a memory box he didn't know he had, a safe

Place where he had deposited echoes and reflections
from long ago, and now he stumbles upon them again

Laying a black jack on a red queen who reclines on the lap
of a black king, stacked up like casualties in the open air

Exhausted angularities in a two-dimensional
orgy of wasted time. From that jack-in-the box coffin

Souls escape in a brace of parting breaths that are never
ever coming back. It's as though relaxing the brain's tight

Fist lets slip get-out-of-jail-free cards to ev'ry screwball
in there, where supposedly securely straightjacketed

And serenely medicated inmates bubble up like drowned
corpses, having (Christ-like) kicked bloody spikes from between

Metatarsals and metacarpals, leaving only bright
stigmata to rise to the surface with a split grin like

That of the great Roman general, Rictus Sardonicus
disciple of blood-thirsty Mars, protector of SPQR

Unresolved conflicts? Things out of kilter? Panic buttons?
the French have words for such curses and cures: *ennui, Drôlerie*

Tristesse, eau de vie, La Vie en Rose, and *solitaire*
odds and ends of fears and desires, almost-accidents

That never happened but haunt us as though they had. Moments
of relative significance and insufficient prayer

For everyone but us. One day he'll quit this useless game
these fruitless entertainments, like smoking and blood-letting

Two-and-a-half-minute increments of his life dropping
extinguished into the abyss. He swears he'll quit when he

Beats the game in under two minutes, all twenty-eight cards
of the original deal distributed into four

Neat stacks of rusted Spades, memories of smoky Clubs, lost
diamondless engagement rings, and thirteen broken Hearts

Unlike Little Susie he never considered himself
the King of the Underground but that's where he reposes

Surprised by death as he was by life, smiling to himself
amidst the pair of crucified jokers. You can almost

Hear their capped bells and juggled suits of red and black hitting
the floor, poor fellows, cheeks in palms, fools in parinirvana.

THE HUBRIS OF INTENTIONAL DEFECT

The hubris of those artists and craftsmen
who build a defect into their work
in deference to the jealous god or gods—

as though without it their work would have
the defect of perfection, ah!

THE WHEEL AND THE BALL

We all know how the wheel was conceived
a maverick slice of lemon rolling

Out of control. The wheel did not evolve
but appeared, complete in design, in style

Entire, like Athena from her father's brow
tread already much advanced, spoked, stoked

And ready to go. But some still say it was
discovered like fire, or in the flip of a coin

When some world-circumnavigator gazed
at the horizon and concluded that

The essence of round was flat. But why did
anyone bother to invent the ball

Who thought of that? Who first bounced the idea
around? Who first announced, *From now on we*

Will no longer play billiards with hollow cue balls
that drift and float, ping and pong. We'll play silly

Golf with them instead. Or was it nostalgia
for a perfect soap bubble that had burst

Foreseen in crystal and thus foretold?
was it a new way to encompass the globe

A narcissistic projection of the eye
dreamt into being for profit or sport?

Was the modern ball an improvement on eggs
onions, coconuts, barbarian skulls

Or any orb wrapped in hair and covered
in skin, one that might not burst when batted

Yet provide exercise to tone not brain
but belly and butt? An excuse to go

Bowling for beers with buddies? To expand
lung and strengthen heart? Or simply a novel

Way of carrying air, an art performed
in a certain season. We are never

Given the reason. Maybe the first ball
was a fortunate goof, a failed attempt

To *imperfect* the perfect Platonic sphere
whatever the truth, whatever fool theory

I suspect the ball was simply man's proof
that the world is small and that he was here.

DECOMPOSITION

Time makes it so
swallowing us whole

Saturn's hunger
for his children

There is only one real sin
among so many minor others

And that is wasted time
daily, hourly, yearly

Minute by minute
no second chance

Even the elements
are constantly at their jobs

In the economy of nature
labor never gets a holiday

Munching away at metal
iron and bronze become

Mere autumnal rust
or artistic verdigris patinas

Rotting hardwoods soon turn
to soft mossy greens

The biosphere reeks
of composting carcasses

Vexing vegetation and flesh
finances and long-lost loves

Yea, even Plato's ιδέες are subject
to eternal decomposition.

THE UPSIDE OF CLIMATE CHANGE

This incessant rain seems unnatural
here in Tennessee

as though Oregon skies got lost, lurking
far from their northwestern home.

After almost a year of malingering
Arizonish drought

for weeks now the warm winter atmosphere
has been bursting

but now the full moon has come to chase
the clouds away

stars have fallen to frost the leafy fields
and meadowgrass again.

It means the thirty thirsty waterfalls
will be replenished,

it means the thousand wells and wellsprings
will have grown fat,

and the pregnant earth all over the mountain
can say *fuck you* to fires.

TORNADO WARNING

Last night we hid from the weather in a closet
taking it seriously, though only for a moment
taking the moment to muse on loss
to imagine the erasure of our lives
to raze the house and garden in our minds
and to levitate the new mailbox—
our cars took flight with witches on bicycle-brooms
a screen door like a playing card sliced a funnel cloud
snake oil salesmen floated by—
we listened for the oncoming train to wreck us
imagined the unbuilding of what we have built
envisioned what our absence will be like:
how uprooted trees shall tumble like dominoes
and shake the cosmic order ground up around us;
how the indiscriminate sowing of seed will then spread
and regenerate the diversity of the ecosystem without us,
reclaiming the ordered chaos that is theirs
has always been theirs and will
always be theirs
amen.

It was soon over—
weather here in Tennessee threatens a different order of
destruction from the one where we're from—a sudden blow,
a swift deconstruction—so unlike hurricanes
whose warnings we're used to, announcing their arrival
like an invading army well in advance,
giving us time to abandon the field to the plunderer,
giving us pause to consider the irresistible might of her forces,
time to ponder the wisdom of flight and surrender,
unconditional capitulation to avoid complete debellation,
time to imagine in its aftermath the lingering death and decay,
giving us time not to hide from but to fly from total devastation

and even to make plans about how we might rebuild
after our return from our extended hurrication
in the wake of Katrina or Rita, Ida or Georges.

With hurricanes, you see, it's personal.
But tornadoes are like a one-night stand:
nameless and—
unless they dismember you like Eros
in one fell swoop,
ripping off your roof
or sweeping you off your foundation—
forgettable.

BORN IN 1952

Eugene, Oregon

I was born in 1952, a year most stellar
ten years after the book *Old Yeller*

when England first heard *The Goon Show*
which revolutionized radio

with Spike Milligan and Peter Sellers
spawning a generation of funny fellers

and who could forget *Singin' in the Rain*
with Gene Kelly higher on love than cocaine

and to think: I was just minus seven
when Hiroshima was sent to heaven.

Let's hope we all make it to 2052,
not me, maybe, but you and you and you.

A CERTAINTY

With the death of every loved one we ask:
Why am *I* still here?
They were better than me, more deserving
of another year.

Yet on we go after each funeral
with a happy face.
I am pretty sure, though, that when I go,
the world will be a better place.

Postface

*AT RIGHT IS THE DEMON NURARIHYON,
IN THE GUISE OF AN OLD MAN WITH A
HUGE HEAD AND BUDDHIST ROSARY. HE IS
FOLLOWED BY RODENT-LIKE MONSTERS.*

THE AROMA OF ANGELS

—from a letter by H. L. Mencken

I continue to disintegrate
gradually and politely.

Towards the close of foggy afternoons,
I can hear the rustle of angels' wings,
and even smell the angels.

It may interest you to know
that their aroma is not unlike that
of turkeys. I suppose that they are

edible, though I can't recall finding
any account in the literature of any
Christian venturing to try them.

ABOUT THE AUTHOR

Photo: Leigh Collins

RICHARD COLLINS taught at universities in the U.S., Wales, Romania, and Bulgaria, before retiring as Dean Emeritus of Arts and Humanities at California State University Bakersfield. He taught for a decade at LSU (where he was the first faculty advisor for *New Delta Review*) and a decade at Xavier University of Louisiana as RosaMary Endowed Professor of English (where he edited the *Xavier Review*). He has been a Fulbright researcher in London and a Fulbright senior lecturer in Romania, as well as a Leverhulme Fellow in Wales. His books include *John Fante: A Literary Portrait* (Guernica Editions, 2000), *No Fear Zen* (Hohm Press, 2015), *In Search of the Hermaphrodite: A Memoir* (Tough Poets Press, 2024), and *Stone Nest: Poems* (Shanti Arts, 2025). Since 2016 he has been abbot of the New Orleans Zen Temple and now resides in Sewanee, Tennessee, where he directs Stone Nest Zen Dojo.